EUROPEAN
INTERIOR DESIGN
THROUGH
THE AGES

uniform with this volume

ENGLISH ARCHITECTURE
THROUGH THE AGES
Secular Building
Leonora and Walter Ison

BRITISH FURNITURE
THROUGH THE AGES
illustrated by Maureen Stafford ARCA
edited with an introduction by
Robert Keith Middlemass

BRITISH DOMESTIC DESIGN
THROUGH THE AGES
Brian Keogh and Melvyn Gill

This book is to be returned on or before the last date stamped below.

EUROPEAN
INTERIOR DESIGN
THROUGH
THE AGES

ANTHONY SULLY
Edited by JEFFREY DANIELS

ARTHUR BARKER LIMITED
5 Winsley Street London W1

SBN 213 17802 8

Unwin Brothers Limited
Woking and London

Introduction

The assembly hall of a school, the living-room of a private house or flat and the lounge of an air-terminal each fulfils a particular function, and is therefore designed in an appropriate way. This appropriateness usually extends from function to appearance, so that on entering a room we know almost immediately what it is for, and therefore how to respond. Clearly this would not matter to a revolutionary mob bursting into a royal palace, but to the courtiers who attached great importance to such a nicety as whether they were allowed inside the balustrade around the monarch's bed, the precise significance of each ante-room in an *enfilade*, or series, was crucially important.

Nevertheless, all rooms have one basic feature, in that they enclose and define space. The ways in which this has been done in Europe during the last 2,000 years or so is the purpose of this collection of illustrations, which have been chosen as far as possible in order to show interiors which are not only representative of the era in which they were created, but which have intrinsic merit as designs. It is often objected that churches, palaces, castles and monumental public buildings tend to get a disproportionate amount of attention in books on architecture, but this is because only the rich and powerful could afford to build to last, and until very recently the vast majority of men and women lived with their families in simple dwellings of no architectural distinction. The horses of an eighteenth-century European nobleman were far more comfortably housed than the labourers who worked in his fields, many of whom were still serfs, bound to remain on the estate where they were born, and often paying over half their miserable earnings in various forms of taxation. They had little time or inclination for interior design!

In such primitive dwellings as the caves of Lascaux (France) and Altamira (Spain) the animals painted on the walls and ceilings were intended to give the tribe power over the actual animals, which were hunted for food. More sophisticated societies assert control over their environment without such magical intentions, but sometimes even more ambitiously. At Würzburg (Germany) for example, the great Venetian decorative painter G.B. Tiepolo was commissioned in 1752 to paint on the staircase ceiling of the magnificent new palace the gods of Olympus and the four continents paying homage to its proud builder, the otherwise quite insignificant Prince-Bishop. On a more modest scale most individuals want to impress their personalities on their surroundings, even if only to the extent of pinning cuttings from the colour supplements on to a board above the bed.

The Tiepolo ceiling at Würzburg was intended to impress by its brilliance, and also by its unexpectedness, although the rich treatment of the palace exterior clearly prepares the visitor for something grand inside. The idea that the walls of a building should link the inside with the outside seems to alternate with the idea that they should perform the opposite function, that of separating them. The great cathedrals of the Middle Ages, with their huge windows and their elaborate scaffolding of flying buttresses, make us aware from the outside what is happening inside, at least structurally, and once we know that the flying buttresses take the thrust of the stone vaults, the logic of these buildings is clear, even if we are only aware of the achievement once we enter.

The buildings of the Renaissance usually belong to the other type, whose walls seem to separate rather than unite exterior and interior. The most extreme example is the *studiolo* of the Grand Duke Francesco de' Medici, built 1570–5 in the Palazzo Vecchio, Florence, Italy: its walls are completely lined with pictures, one of which opens to reveal a window, and others, doors to various secret chambers and even a staircase down to the street. When all the panels are closed, however, there is no natural source of light and no discernible exit.

Nowadays, with modern methods of construction based on a framework rather than solid load-bearing walls, we are back to the Gothic see-through system. Large picture windows make the view outside a room a feature of the decoration, although when that view is merely someone else's picture window, there seems little point.

The factor which we have called appropriateness is perhaps the key one in thinking about interior design, and in a society as technically resourceful as our own, it is closely linked with choice, a privilege which in earlier times was restricted to a small minority. When we look at interiors from different epochs, created by various forms of society, we must bear in mind the activities they were intended to enclose. The saloon of Queen Victoria's railway carriage looks like a rather over-furnished drawing-room on wheels, thus giving the Queen the illusion that she was still comfortably at home.

Man's earliest buildings were primarily built to shelter the occupants. Construction was primitive, and wattle and daub techniques for hut building were common. As man's social, spiritual and cultural background developed so civilizations began to emerge. The two thousand years of relative peace the Egyptians experienced provided them with the opportunity of creating a well conceived and solid foundation to their architecture and decoration. As the Egyptians were great navigators who sent their ships to all ports of the Mediterranean Sea, the early tribes of Greece and its islands, together with the primitive inhabitants of the Spanish and Italian peninsulas, felt their cultural influence.

The sea-based Minoan civilization, which had spread from the island of Crete to the mainland, was destroyed in the twelfth century BC by warlike tribes who became known as the Greeks when they settled in the valleys and coastal areas of that mountainous peninsular. By the end of the seventh century BC the Greeks were building stone temples, eventually providing future generations with the basic classical orders which became universal in their application. The Greeks desired to attain perfection in all accomplishments, no matter how great or small. This attitude is evident in the great heights achieved in philosophy, literature and the fine arts. They regarded wisdom and physical beauty as the great human attributes. Man was the measure of all things, hence their conception of gods and goddesses as perfect human beings, although, unlike the Egyptians, they were not dominated by their religion. Temples were, however, at first the only stone buildings, but later theatres, law-courts and colonnaded shelters around market-places were built on a monumental scale. The materials used externally and internally were marble and limestone which took a very high polish on the surface. Ornament was carved in relief, and with other forms of decoration related closely to the structure rather than being vaguely applied as surface decoration.

The Romans were primarily colonisers, organisers and lawgivers. Being an extremely practical people they did not have the creative genius that the Greeks possessed. While they were conquering countries such as Carthage, Macedonia, Greece, Asia Minor, Spain, Syria, Egypt and Britain during the years 146–31 BC, they were steadily importing all Greek ideas. Because of the shortage of Roman craftsmen they eventually had to import Greek craftsmen as well to carry out work such as the building of Rome. The great period of Roman building occurred between the years 100 BC and AD 300. They used their imagination in adapting Greek thought to new engineering concepts in building, as well as to new decorative concepts inside and outside the building. The column was no longer used exclusively on a purely functional basis, but was applied to walls in relief as decoration, as for example on the Colosseum, Rome, built at the end of the first century AD. Their main contribution to architecture was their extensive use of the arch, the vault and the dome. Materials used in decoration included alabaster, porphyry, jasper, and mosaics of glass and coloured stones and inlaid marble. Walls were often painted in fresco, and stucco (plaster) relief ornament was also frequently applied. The high degree of perfection attained can still be studied in the splendid interiors at Pompeii and Herculaneum, near Naples, Italy.

When the power and dominance of Rome began to fade, the various countries of Europe were each developing the inheritance of ideas and religious beliefs in their own way. The most important event to occur at this time was the advent of Christianity. Under Constantine, the first Christian Emperor, the seat of Empire was removed from Rome to Byzantium, which led to the development of a new style of church. Church architecture became prominent because the Christian Church was the only power which managed to keep its authority in a disintegrating world. At Constantinople the church of Santa Sophia (AD 532–7) combines a huge dome with tunnel-vaults to create the most impressive achievement of Byzantine art. At the same time, in the West, important churches were being built at Ravenna, on the east coast of Italy. These churches closely followed the plan of the basilica, or Roman hall of justice, and were lavishly decorated with mosaics. The Eastern and Western Empires, temporarily reunited in the sixth century, were finally separated in 752 when the Lombards overran Italy, but not until 1453, when the Turks captured Constantinople, was the last link with Imperial Rome broken.

In the West, intellectual life virtually ceased to exist as tribal warfare raged on, and countless leaders endeavoured to establish their supremacy.

Charlemagne finally won through and became the great early patron of the arts in Western Europe. The gradual development of the Feudal System in Europe eventually combined in about AD 1000 with a reforming movement in the monasteries of Eastern France to produce a style of architecture which we call Romanesque. Its characteristic achievements are the great churches and abbeys of the Rhineland, South-West France and Britain, with their massive walls, semicircular arches and bold, vigorous decoration. The castles of Norman England represent the secular equivalent.

The beginning of the Gothic style can be precisely dated and located: AD 1140, at St Denis, near Paris, in the area known as the Île de France. A brilliant but unknown master-mason thought of using pointed arches combined with ribbed vaults and flying buttresses to create a stone skeleton based on a balance of thrusts, which produced stability without massiveness. The builders of Durham Cathedral at the end of the eleventh century had shown the way, but it was the example of St Denis that was taken up in both France and England, making possible the marvels of Amiens and Rheims, Salisbury and Lincoln. English builders skilfully exploited the tremendous possibilities of the Gothic style, and English architecture between 1250 and 1350 has been described as 'the most forward, the most important and the most inspired in Europe'.

The Crusades (1096–1270) were of great political, economic and cultural significance. The eastward march brought the crusaders into contact with materials such as the silk textiles of Damascus, Mosul and Alexandria; the exquisite glassware of Tyre and the jewels and pearls of Byzantine and Mohammedan merchants. These rich products were all brought back to furnish the homes of Western Europe. The influence of the Crusades on castle-building was considerable, as Edward I's castles in Wales demonstrate by their concentric and symmetrical plans.

The fourteenth century witnessed the greatest disaster of the Middle Ages, the Black Death, which swept across Europe in the 1340's. In spite of this, living standards were beginning to rise especially in the towns where trade was encouraged by more settled political conditions, and a sophisticated court life developed in important administrative centres like London, Avignon and Prague. It is however true that the mass of the population dwelt in crude cottages constructed of local materials.

The Gothic style spread only to the Northern parts of Italy, and in Venice a unique fusion with Byzantine elements created the sumptuous palaces of which the best known is the Cà d'Oro. By the fifteenth century the wealth that had been brought to Italy by its trade became concentrated in the hands of several distinct groups who also grasped political and ecclesiastical control. Each city and town was dominated by one or more leading families, such as the Medici, Pitti, Strozzi and Riccardi of Florence; the Visconti and later the Sforza of Milan; the Colonna, Borgia, Orsini and Borghese of Rome; and the Vendramini, Foscari, Mocenigo and Contarini of Venice. The word 'Renaissance' is used as the name of the intellectual movement that resulted in the revival of classical philosophy and art, beginning in Florence about the year 1400. The early period in

Italy lasted until about 1500, when Rome took over from Florence as the most important centre of artistic activity. The sack of Rome (1527) scattered the artists and impoverished their patrons, but ultimately led to the spread of the Renaissance throughout Europe.

Renaissance influence appeared in Spanish architecture after the conquest of Granada (1492), the last Moslem state in Spain. In France it began about 1530 during the reign of Francis I, and in the Netherlands and Germany towards the end of the sixteenth century. England followed France in receiving foreign influences which were mixed with the late Gothic style. All European countries to a large extent depended upon the availability of Italian artists and craftsmen. Artists in many fields travelled widely at this time, establishing a recognizable court-style which we call Mannerism. Palaces and villas, as well as the churches and cathedrals, became the object of attention for the creative talents of architects, painters, sculptors and craftsmen. The religious upheavals of the period did not prevent the building of new churches, and it was in fact to help to pay for the re-building of St Peter's, Rome, that the sale of Indulgences was encouraged by the Papacy, rousing Luther to the outburst that precipitated the Reformation.

The seventeenth century was the golden age for France and the time when the conflict between Gothic survivals and the classic orders was determined and a national style established. The arts flourished under King Henry IV who considered their encouragement a matter of state policy. The basically domestic manner of the first half of the century gave way to a cold, grand version of the Baroque style during the long reign of Louis XIV. The work that symbolises the feeling of France in the second half of the century is the vast palace of Versailles by Le Vau and Jules Hardouin Mansart. The gardens and park were laid out by André le Nôtre. Gianlorenzo Bernini was called in from Italy to design extensions to the Louvre which were never actually carried out.

Italy was the home of the Baroque style at its most successful, and Bernini's sweeping colonnades in front of St Peter's, Rome, fully express its essential qualities – movement, drama and superhuman scale. Bernini's rival was the neurotic Borromini, whose influence extended far beyond Rome to Sicily at the Southern tip of Italy, Piedmont in the north, and ultimately through Nicholas Hawksmoor to England.

The seventeenth century in England was the age of Inigo Jones and Sir Christopher Wren, who each established a personal style based on a correct understanding of the classical elements of architecture, having made independent studies of Italian and French designs. In the latter part of the century after the Restoration (1660) the work of Grinling Gibbons became popular and his carvings seem almost to become an essential part of the interior decoration of the time. He took most aspects of nature's plants and fruit as his themes as well as satisfying demands for more formal work such as coats of arms. Gibbons carved mainly in lime-wood, which showed up well against the dark oak panelling, but he also worked in stone and bronze.

The Baroque style is the natural expression of strong monarchy and the

Roman Church, but nonetheless it reached Protestant Holland through the work of Daniel Marot and England through a group of architects associated with Wren about 1700. As well as Hawksmoor, already mentioned, Sir John Vanbrugh and Thomas Archer made important contributions to the creation of a brief but powerful phase in English architecture.

In Spain the Baroque manner gave the nation a chance to reveal their talent for decoration which carried through until the eighteenth century, and is sometimes known as Churrigueresque.

The cultural pre-eminence of France continued into the eighteenth century, and the Baroque style entered its final phase, the Rococo. Deriving from the shell-work popular in the grottoes of seventeenth-century gardens, the Rococo was primarily a way of decorating interiors either with carved wood panelling or moulded plaster ornamentation. Asymmetrical designs were extensively used and straight lines were carefully avoided, creating an atmosphere of delicate refinement ideally suited to the frivolous and pleasure-loving court of Louis XV. The style was extremely popular in Austria and Southern Germany, where it was applied not only to palaces and pavilions, but rather surprisingly, to churches as well. Frederick the Great's palace of Sans-Souci at Potsdam in North Germany is a late example of a style which had only limited success in England, but was widely adopted in Italy.

By about 1750 a new conception of architectural design was being discussed in Paris, Rome and London. This looked back beyond the Renaissance to the classical world, as revealed in Greek vases (thought to be Etruscan), the ruins of the monuments of both Greeks and Romans and above all the evidence of Graeco-Roman interior decoration made available by the recent discovery of Pompeii and later, Herculaneum. Neoclassicism, as it is called, is the first self-conscious European style, and its influence soon affected not only architecture but also painting, furniture and even dress. The Louis XVI style in France, the Adam style in England are both derived from the new movement, which reached its culmination after the French Revolution in the so-called Empire style of the early nineteenth century.

Enlightened patronage by a wealthy, highly educated, self-confident aristocracy encouraged artists and craftsmen to produce work of the highest standard, even if it favoured the conventionally acceptable rather than the obstinately original. The Grand Tour undertaken by every Englishman of rank and wealth helped to keep England in touch with the ideas and taste of France and Italy, a link that was unfortunately severed by the Revolutionary and Napoleonic wars.

The nineteenth century in England began with the Regency period, which marked the beginning of a decline in general design standards. Originality gave way to a resurgence of past decorative motifs applied at random to objects and interiors as mere ornament, rather than being used with thought for the origin of detail or the relevance to its intended function. Sir George Gilbert Scott summed up the Victorian attitude by asserting that the great principle of architecture was 'to decorate construction'. The revival of Gothic and Renaissance styles seemed to contradict what was happening on the industrial scene, where new social functions were born of invention and discovery. Plentiful supplies of hitherto expensive materials like iron and glass pointed the way to new methods of construction, which were only gradually adopted by 'serious' architects. The Crystal Palace (1851) and the great station sheds for the new railways were designed by men who were primarily engineers.

Some designers welcomed the challenge of industrial development, but others were unsympathetic to the machine, and chose to follow the crafts movement, led by William Morris. The writings of John Ruskin did much to elucidate the theory behind the motivation of Morris and his followers. The English domestic style of the twentieth century was founded on the work of men like Philip Webb, Norman Shaw, W.R. Lethaby and C.F.A. Voysey.

The most interesting product of the late nineteenth century is the Art Nouveau style of which Victor Horta and Henri Van de Velde were the main practitioners in Belgium, where its impact was profound and widespread. C.R. Mackintosh in Scotland and Gaudí in Spain pursued the same feelings but in very different ways.

So far the twentieth century has seen the greatest number of changes over the shortest possible time in the history of Europe. All aspects of life have developed so fast that a tight control on communication methods has become an important factor in everyday life. Because of the complex nature of relationships in business and domestic life, the attainment of clarity rather than confusion, order rather than chaos, demands constant effort. The contemporary designer has to contend with a thousand pressures newly created by the material advancement of man.

By 1914 the younger designers had broken with the past and had accepted the machine age with all its new discoveries and inventions. The Bauhaus in Germany expounded a whole new philosophy of design, which has influenced designers ever since. Perret of France, Le Corbusier of Switzerland and France, Behrens, Mendelsohn, Breuer and Gropius of Germany, Oud of Holland, Klint of Denmark and Asplund of Sweden were amongst the pioneers of the architecture that is built today. Eero Saarinen, Alvar Aalto, Adelbert Niemeyer, Pier Luigi Nervi, Denys Lasdun and Sir Hugh Casson have all developed an architecture closely related to function, and their buildings reveal the age they were built in.

What of the future? How will the designer help to create the environment of the 1970's? The air is full of systems, methods, programmes, and computerised techniques, which clearly indicate a way ahead. The idea of 'plug-in' living cells to press-button controlled environment is being seriously discussed. Knock-down furniture packed and supplied as a kit of parts to be assembled by the receiver is already accepted.

In any case, we can no longer think of Europe as a separate, independent culture. Exciting new developments in design are happening all over the world, in places like Brasilia and Chandigarh, where new cities are rising to create an environment appropriate to the rising standard of life which all men today rightly want to achieve.

Greek, Roman and Byzantine

Painted decoration of a high standard of naturalism was a feature of the great palace of Knossos, Crete, whose hundreds of rooms and passages created the labyrinth which is the setting for the famous Greek legend of Theseus and the Minotaur. The columns, which taper downwards, were originally brightly painted too, as can be seen in the restored parts of the palace. Formal designs were used as borders round openings.

Greek temples were once also brightly painted in glowing colours, which have long since worn away, leaving the natural stone or marble in all their beauty. The religious ceremonies of the Greeks, like those of the Romans, took place outside the temples, and the *cella* was a dimly-lit room roofed with cedar-wood and containing the gold and ivory-plated statue of the god or goddess to whom the temple was dedicated.

Unlike the Greeks, whose buildings rely on beautiful proportions for their effect, the Romans loved opulent decoration, favouring an ostentatious magnificence that we should probably have found vulgar. The great public baths of Rome and other important cities of the Empire were vast in scale, complex in plan and lavish in decoration, as their many imposing ruins still demonstrate. The Pantheon, Rome, built as a temple to all the gods, is the only ancient building to preserve its original dome, whose inner surface is decorated with sunken panels: this is known as coffering. Houses and villas often contained rooms beautifully frescoed with landscapes, scenes from the lives of the gods, or complicated architectural fantasies almost like stage-sets. Hadrian's villa at Tivoli had a summer dining-room surrounded by a moat and looking into a garden containing statues and fountains.

The early Christians decorated their first churches very modestly, but as Christianity became more powerful, so churches were more sumptuously adorned. Pagan temples were torn down, and the columns used to support the arcades of basilicas. Mosaic pictures and patterns glowed with gold and rich colours, and the light was sometimes filtered through thin panels of selenite, as at the basilica of Santa Sabina, Rome. The most splendid mosaics survive at Ravenna, but there are fine, slightly later ones in the same style, at St Mark's, Venice, and at the cathedral of Monreale, near Palermo, Sicily.

Outside Italy, the most notable buildings were those erected by the Arab conquerors of Southern Spain, as the graceful horseshoe arches of the mosque at Cordova clearly indicate. An important oasis of cultural activity in the uncouth wastes of Northern Europe was Charlemagne's capital at Aix-la-Chapelle, where the chapel of his palace still survives as part of the cathedral.

Romanesque

Among the buildings which have survived from the 150 years of confusion and barbarism which followed the death of Charlemagne is an important group of churches with a 'westwork' built on at the end of the nave. The ground-floor of this tower-like structure is usually vaulted, while the upper floors communicate directly with the nave by means of arcades. The abbey church at Corvey-on-the-Weser, Germany, has a fine example of such a westwork. The precise function of these westworks is not clear.

Carolingian elements in design lingered on, sometimes combined with Byzantine features, as in the Convent Church of S. Cyriacus, Gernrode, Saxony, Germany.

The Viking raiders who settled in Normandy had by the eleventh century become relatively civilized, and their influence was felt in England at the court of Edward the Confessor even before the momentous invasion of 1066. The Norman cathedrals, abbeys and castles in England are among the chief glories of the Romanesque style in all its simple grandeur. The Chapel of St John in the White Tower of the Tower of London is still completely unspoilt, and the cathedral at Durham has the distinction of being roofed with the first ribbed high vault in Europe, thus foreshadowing the development of the Gothic style.

In the South-West of France a series of magnificent churches is evidence of the creative vitality of the twelfth century. At Angoulême, the single nave is broken up into a series of domed bays, and at Périgueux, the church of St Front is also roofed with domes, but is centrally planned, like a Greek cross (i.e. with four equal arms), on the lines of St Mark's, Venice.

Italian Romanesque can be seen at its simplest at the church of San Pietro, Agliate, near Milan, and at its most elaborate at Pisa, in the Cathedral, the Baptistry and the famous leaning Tower.

The interiors of Romanesque buildings, generally stark and unadorned, were sometimes relieved by the use of monumental sculpture, as at the church of the Magdalen at Vézelay, France. On festive occasions the churches were decorated with embroidered hangings, like the celebrated Bayeux Tapestry which was used to adorn the Cathedral at Bayeux in Normandy.

Domestic interiors were characteristic of a tough, harsh age, and if the huge wall-fireplaces indicate some concession to comfort, the thick stone walls and glassless shuttered windows must have provided fierce competition. In Sicily, however, which the Normans conquered in the twelfth century, they embellished the Royal Palace at Palermo with beautiful mosaic ceiling decorations, those in the Hall of King Roger portraying lively hunting scenes.

Greek, Roman Byzantine and Romanesque

Cave of Lascaux, Dordogne, FRANCE. The paintings on the walls and ceiling were made some thirty thousand years ago. This type of primitive art signified the real presence of the animals portrayed, and served to give the inhabitants an opportunity of exercising power over them.

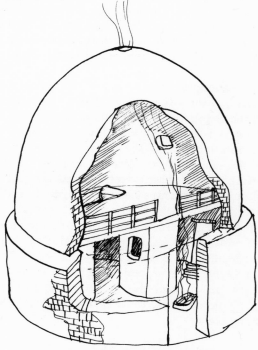

Neolithic house, Khirokitia, CYPRUS

Knossos, CRETE c.2000-1400 BC Caravanserai. This was an Inn outside the southern entrance to the palace

Chamber, Royal Palace

Queen's Megaron (ceremonial hall)

a. Greek Doric

b. Greek Ionic

Temple of Aphaia, Aegina, GREECE 1st half 5th century BC

c. Greek Corinthian

Dining Pavilion, Hadrian's villa, ITALY. 2nd cent. AD

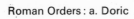

Roman Orders : a. Doric   b. Ionic   c. Corinthian

The Romans elaborated on these producing two other orders, the Tuscan and Composite.

Reconstruction of the frigidarium of Hadrian's baths,
Leptis Magna, Tripolitania, NORTH AFRICA. One of the
most important examples of the communal baths which
were a feature of every Roman town in all parts of the Empire.

Pantheon, Rome, ITALY. Built by Hadrian c.126 AD

Funeral Chapel, New Catacomb of Via Latina, Rome, ITALY. Mid 4th cent. AD

Church of S. Constanza, Rome, ITALY. Early 4th cent AD. Originally a tomb.

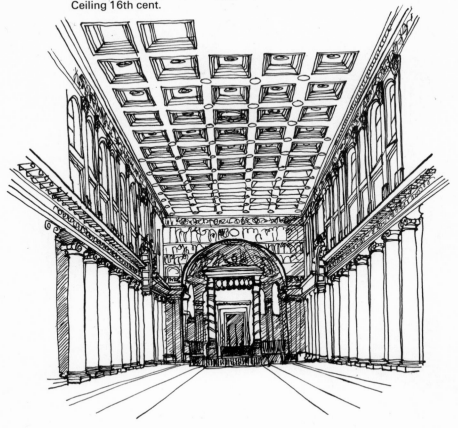

Nave, Basilica of S. Maria Maggiore, Rome, ITALY. c.440 AD.
Ceiling 16th cent.

Nave, S. Sabina, Rome, ITALY. 422-432 AD. The columns
here support two rows of arches and not straight
entablatures.

Basilica of S. Apollinare Nuovo, Ravenna, ITALY. Early 6th cent AD

Mosaic frieze details : a. Christ healing the paralytic.

b. The Last Supper

S. Lorenzo, Milan, ITALY. 370 AD

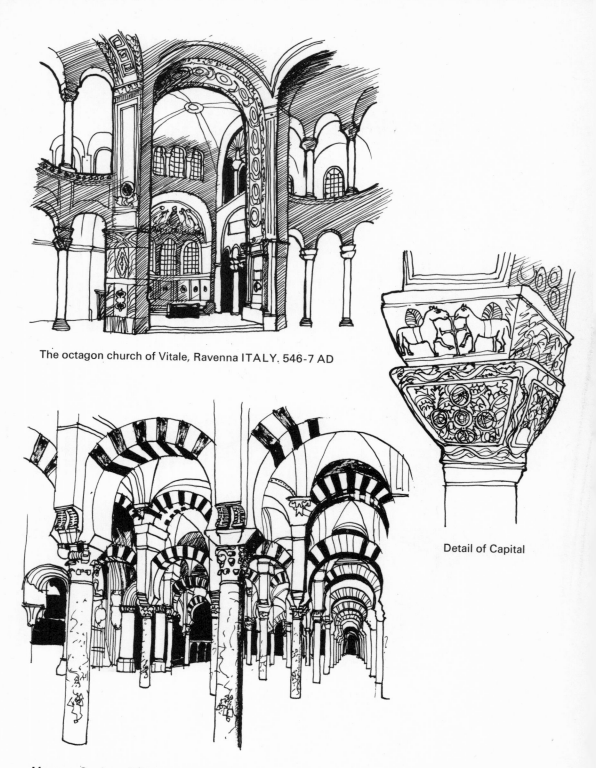

The octagon church of Vitale, Ravenna ITALY. 546-7 AD

Detail of Capital

Mosque, Cordova, SPAIN. 786-990 AD

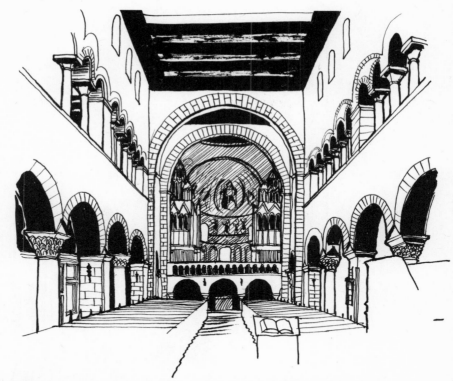

Convent church of S. Cyriacus, Gernrode, Saxony, GERMANY. 963-972

Westwork, Abbey church, Corvey-on-the-Weser. GERMANY. 873-85

Nave, Durham Cathedral, ENGLAND. 1093 – 1130

St John's Chapel, White Tower, Tower of London, ENGLAND. 1078

Cloisters S. Domingo de Silos,
SPAIN. 1074

Church of S. Pietro, Agliate
near Milan, ITALY. Early 11th
cent?

Cross vaults, Abbey church of Maria Leach,
GERMANY. 1100

Nave, Church of S. Savin-sur-Gartempe,
FRANCE. Early 12th cent.

Inner Portal, Church
of the Magdalene,
Vézelay, FRANCE.
c.1130. Tympanum
with carving of the
Pentecost.

Angoulême Cathedral, FRANCE. Early 12th cent.

Capitals, Crypt of Canterbury Cathedral, ENGLAND. c.1110-1130

S. Front in Perigeux, FRANCE, 2nd quarter of 12th cent.

Archivolt of the Porch, Andrieu, FRANCE 12th cent.

Cloister door, St Emmeram, Regensburg, GERMANY. 1230

Gothic

The Gothic church interior is quite different in feeling from the Romanesque: the graceful vaults and slender columns of the ambulatory at the Abbey of St Denis are instantly recognizable as Gothic. Richly coloured stained-glass windows illuminate each altar in this series of chapels constructed round the choir to create the characteristically curved east end of French Gothic churches.

The nave of Sens Cathedral, France, illustrates the early form of Gothic church interior, in which the thrust of the vault is taken by the side aisles, represented internally by the small, dark triforium stage above the main nave arcade. At Laon, begun some sixty years later, the triforium is lit by windows and the side aisles have become two storeys high. Only a small blind arcade separates the enlarged triforium from the windows of the clerestory above, since the nave vaults are supported by properly constructed flying buttresses.

The Romanesque tradition remained strong in Southern France, and in Italy, where contact with the ancient world was never utterly lost. The beautiful interior of the church of San Miniato al Monte, on a hill above Florence, contains re-used capitals from classical columns as well as others carved to match. The walls are faced with panels of marble inlaid with formal designs in dark green and white, while at Siena Cathedral the walls and pillars are given a bold striped treatment. This lavish use of marble is a feature of architecture in Tuscany, an area noted for its stone and marble quarries.

Marble from Purbeck in Dorset was much used in England during the thirteenth century in what is usually called the Early English phase of the Gothic style. It is seen at its finest in Salisbury Cathedral, whose nave is notable for its superb proportions and noble lines. The Decorated phase of English Gothic is as rich as its name implies, but the longest phase is the Perpendicular which was created in the south-west of the country about 1330. The choir of Gloucester Cathedral is an important early instance of a style that was to linger on well into the seventeenth century.

The most attractive domestic interiors of the period are to be found in the English manor houses: Haddon Hall, Derbyshire, Penshurst Place, Kent, and Ightham Mote, also in Kent, are good examples. The Great Hall at Ightham was built about 1340, and retains its original timber roof, although the large window is a fifteenth-century insertion, and the panelling modern.

The Gothic style was basically an Anglo-French creation, although its influence extended into Germany (Cologne Cathedral) and Spain, where the cathedral at Barcelona has close affinities with the one at Albi in the South of France. Both buildings are encircled by a ring of two-storeyed side-chapels, two to each bay at Barcelona.

Gothic

Nave, Walksoken church, Norfolk,
ENGLAND.

Choir, Ambulatory, Abbey of S. Denis,
Paris, FRANCE. 1140-1144

Nave, Sens Cathedral, FRANCE after 1130

Gallery and pulpit,
Modena Cathedral,
ITALY. c.1220

Detail of Capital, S. Martin d'Ainay,
Lyons, FRANCE. 12th cent.

Nave, Laon Cathedral,
FRANCE. 2nd quarter
12th cent.

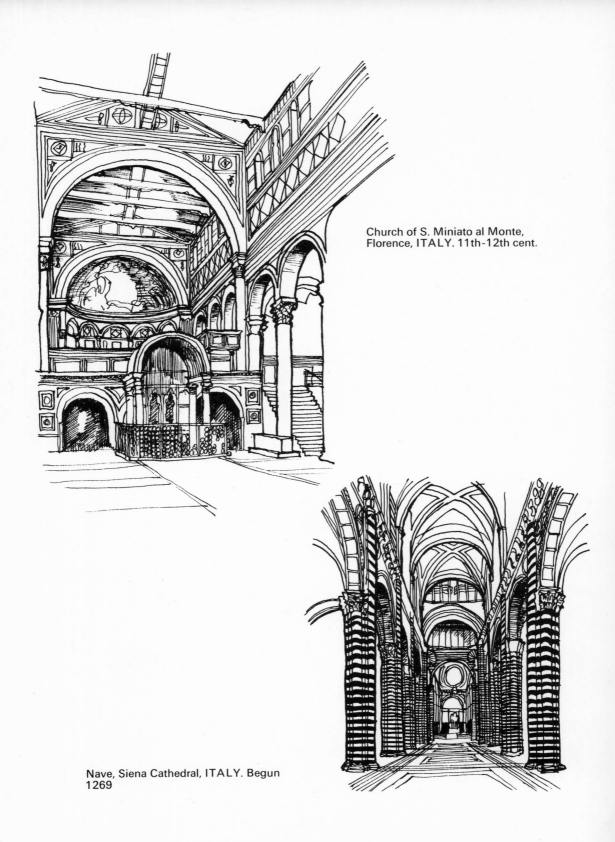

Church of S. Miniato al Monte,
Florence, ITALY. 11th-12th cent.

Nave, Siena Cathedral, ITALY. Begun
1269

Nave, Barcelona Cathedral, SPAIN. Begun 1298

Nave, Salisbury Cathedral,
ENGLAND. Begun 1220

Encaustic tile, Westminster
Abbey floor, ENGLAND.13th
cent.

Chapter House, Salisbury
Cathedral, ENGLAND c.1275

Nave, Exeter Cathedral, ENGLAND. 1280-1370

Choir, Gloucester Cathedral,
ENGLAND. 1337-c.1357

Great Hall, Ightham Mote, Kent,
ENGLAND. 1340

Fifteenth Century

The Italian Renaissance, which was to have a revolutionary effect on architecture and design throughout Europe, was at first confined to the city of Florence. There Filippo Brunelleschi built the cathedral dome, the first in Europe since the days of the Romans. He also designed the exquisite Pazzi Chapel, with its cool, beautifully proportioned interior in dark stone and white painted plaster. The pilasters (flat columns) and their entablature perform the important visual function of defining the separate areas of the interior and at the same time binding them together. In the church of Santo Spirito, also in Florence, he built a basilica-type church with careful attention to correct classical detail, even going so far as to place a section of entablature above each of the columns.

The powerful families of the city-states of Italy often used their wealth to re-build or enlarge their palaces: the Gonzaga at Mantua commissioned Andrea Mantegna to decorate a room in their huge castle with the first recorded illusionistic ceiling painting. The ducal palace further south at Urbino has been described as 'the first royal palace of modern times' since it provided such amenities as bathrooms and a green-house. The interior retains some of its original decoration, including the vaulted ceiling of the Duchess's salon, with its cherubs and garlands in stucco, and the Duke's studio whose walls are lined with wooden panelling marvellously inlaid with scenes in accurate perspective.

The rest of Europe continued to build in the Gothic style, which achieved heights of decorative fantasy and structural daring like the great Perpendicular chapel of King's College Chapel, Cambridge, England, St George's Church, Dinkelsbuhl in South Germany and the pilgrimage church at St Nicholas de Port, Lorraine, France. Architects travelled from Germany to work in Spain, soon to become the proudest and most powerful country in Europe with a vast empire and seemingly unlimited supplies of gold and silver.

England's forests, still large enough to satisfy the demands on them, encouraged the lavish use of timber in building, as even comparatively modest structures like barns dramatically demonstrate. The hall of Great Dixter, Sussex, has a splendid hammer-beam roof, which fully exploits the decorative possibilities of the open type of roof construction. The practice of lining the walls with wooden panelling became current during the latter part of the century, and this made rooms at once warmer and more inviting. It was often embellished with carving, which was an important feature of church interiors throughout the Gothic period.

Pazzi chapel, S. Croce,
Florence, ITALY. 1430-36.
Filippo Brunelleschi

Madonna and child by
Antonio Rosselino
S. Croce.

Church of S. Spirito, Florence,
ITALY. Begun by Filippo
Brunelleschi in 1436, completed to
his designs c.1487

Salon of Duchess' apartment, Ducal Palace of Urbino, ITALY. c.1476

St George's church, Dunkelsbuhl, GERMANY 1444-1499

Aisle, St Nicholas de Port, Lorraine,
FRANCE. 1496

King's College chapel,
Cambridge, ENGLAND.
1512

Barn, Caldecote, Herts, ENGLAND 15th cent.

The Lonja (Exchange), Palma de
Majorca, SPAIN 1426

Chapel of Condestable, Burgos
Cathedral, SPAIN. Simon of
Cologne. 1482

King's chamber, Gatehouse Tower,
Oxburgh Hall, Norfolk, ENGLAND.
c.1482

Chapter House, New Cathedral, Salamanca,
SPAIN. 1500. Juan Gil de Hontañòn

Barn, Tisbury, Wiltshire, ENGLAND 15th cent.

The Hall, Great Dixter, Sussex, ENGLAND c.1450

Gothic details, carving in wood. Late 15th cent.

Kitchen, Hillside Farm, Hepton, Norfolk, ENGLAND. 15th cent.

Sixteenth Century

The Renaissance in Italy spread to Rome largely through two Florentine Popes, Leo X and Clement VII, both members of the Medici family. A brief period of less than thirty years produced the stupendous ceiling of the Sistine Chapel by Michelangelo, and the Vatican Stanze, a suite of Papal apartments painted by his great rival Raphael, who also designed a set of tapestries to hang round the walls of the Sistine Chapel on special occasions. The tradition of painting walls and ceilings with illusionistic decoration was carried on by Giulio Romano in Mantua, by Corregio in Parma and later in the century by Veronese in Venice. The work of Andrea Palladio, from Vicenza, is outstanding for its purity and simplicity, and the austere, light-filled interiors of his two Venetian churches recall Alberti's work in Florence.

In domestic architecture a new room made its appearance; the long gallery, which was intended partly for the display of art treasures and pictures, and partly for indoor exercise and entertainments. The Gallery of Francis I at the Palace of Fontainebleau, France, is one of the most magnificent. It was designed and decorated by Italian artists and craftsmen, many of whom were grateful for the relative security of the French court after the political turmoil of their native land.

The fashion for such galleries spread to northern countries like Scotland and Denmark and no large Elizabethan house in England was complete without one. The staircase became much more prominent in this century, and architects exercised great ingenuity in devising striking and original variations on a basically simple theme. The double-newel staircase at Chambord in France was allegedly based on an idea put forward by Leonardo da Vinci, himself the embodiment of the Renaissance concept of the complete man, as distinguished a scientist as he was an artist.

The ideas and stylistic motifs of the Renaissance were also spread throughout Europe by printed books, whose crude wood-engravings coarsened the original designs almost beyond recognition. If we compare the purity of Michelangelo's staircase at the Laurentian Library, Florence, with the charming but utterly inaccurate screen in the hall at Montacute House, Somerset, England, we can at once see that the message has become distorted; in other words, the Elizabethan design is provincial.

Sixteenth Century

The Big Hall, showing Minstrel's gallery, Compton Wynyates,
Warwickshire, ENGLAND 15th cent. Roof reconstructed 1512.
Screen early 16th c.

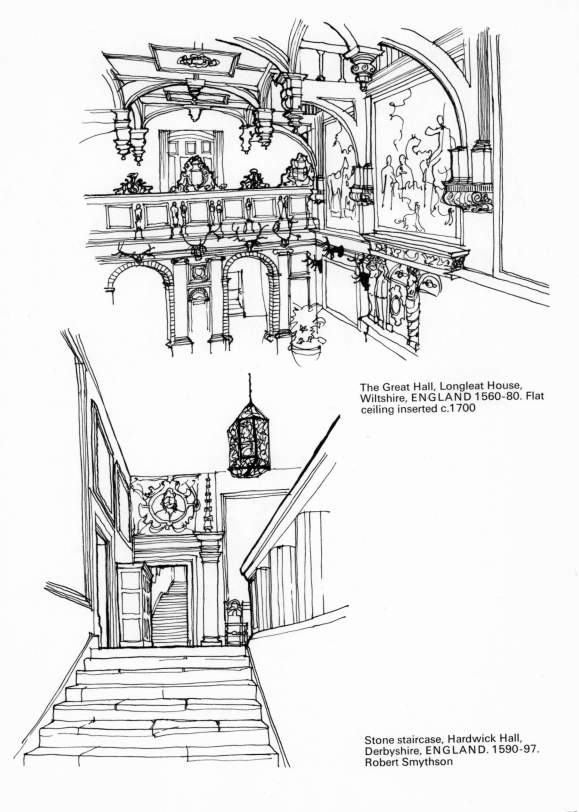

The Great Hall, Longleat House,
Wiltshire, ENGLAND 1560-80. Flat
ceiling inserted c.1700

Stone staircase, Hardwick Hall,
Derbyshire, ENGLAND. 1590-97.
Robert Smythson

Chevy Chase, St Michael's Mt, Cornwall, ENGLAND. This room takes its name from the frieze of scenes of the chase. Formerly a monk's refectory.

Arms of St Aubyn and Godolphin in above. After 1657.

The Long Gallery, Crathes castle, Kincardinshire, SCOTLAND. 1553-95.
The oak panelled ceiling is unique in Scotland.

Gallery of Francis I, Fontainbleau, FRANCE. 1534-40. By Rosso
Fiorentino and assistants.

Double Newel staircase, Castle of Chambord, FRANCE. After 1519

Guard room, Castle of Chateaudun, FRANCE. After 1511

A room in Philip II's private apartments, The Escorial. SPAIN. Juan Bautista de Toledo and Juan de Herrera.

Hall of Swans, Sintra Palace, PORTUGAL. The painted ceiling dates from c.1430 but the characteristic tiled surrounds to windows and doors were added 100 years later. The chairs are 18th cent.

Great Hall, Kronberg castle, DENMARK. Said to be the largest hall in northern Europe. 200ft.

Entrance Hall, Castle of Egeskov, DENMARK. After 1545 by Martin Bussert.

Vestibule of Laurentian Library, S. Lorenzo, Florence, ITALY. 1523-34
Michaelangelo

Stone screen, Great Hall, Montacute, Somerset,
ENGLAND. 1600. William Arnold

S. Giorgio Maggiore, Venice, ITALY 1565. Palladio

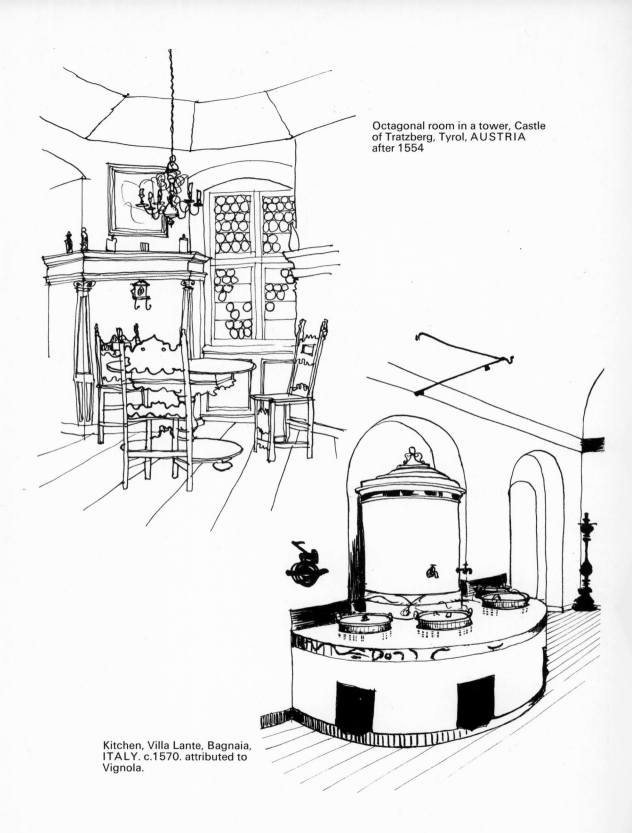

Octagonal room in a tower, Castle
of Tratzberg, Tyrol, AUSTRIA
after 1554

Kitchen, Villa Lante, Bagnaia,
ITALY. c.1570. attributed to
Vignola.

Seventeenth Century

In Italy the patronage of the Popes became once more of great significance, and the Barberini Pope, Urban VIII, deliberately set out to surpass his Renaissance predecessors. His favourite architect was Gianlorenzo Bernini, who enriched the interior of St Peter's, Rome, by designing a baldacchino (canopy to cover the high altar) made from the bronze beams of the Pantheon. Urban also had a huge palace built for himself in Rome, whose ballroom was frescoed by Pietro da Cortona. Another Pope, Innocent X, also employed Pietro to decorate a ceiling in his family palace, in a long gallery designed by Borromini. This architect's most important works are all religious, and the tiny church of San Carlo alle Quatro Fontane, Rome, is a perfect expression of his genius, with its diamond-shaped plan and undulating walls with their deliberately over-large columns and coffered apses in false perspective. Bernini was always much more straightforwardly dramatic, but no less skilful, as in his celebrated Royal Staircase from St Peter's into the Vatican Palace, Rome, where he makes the columns smaller towards the top in order to make it look longer.

Bernini visited France in 1665, but his designs for the Louvre were considered to be both impractical and lacking in that restraint which the French considered essential, and were able to find in architects like François Mansart and Claude Perrault, the latter of whom built the much-discussed extensions to the Louvre. The decoration of Louis XIV's chief monument, the Palace of Versailles, was entrusted to a group of artists and craftsmen working under the general guidance of Charles Le Brun, who favoured lavish use of richly-coloured marbles, large mirrors and much gilding of carved and moulded ornament.

French taste in decoration was imitated after 1660 in England, where Louis XIV's cousins, Charles II and James II, ruled successively. In the earlier part of the century Inigo Jones achieved distinction as the first English architect who really understood what the Renaissance was about, and the interior of Wilton House, near Salisbury, gives some idea of his style.

Sir Christopher Wren met Bernini briefly in 1665, but French influence is more noticeable in his work. His most beautiful church, St Stephen's, Walbrook, London, is a masterpiece of three-dimensional geometry, which produces a harmony that not even the crude modern stained-glass can wreck.

Italian and French painters continued to travel around Europe in search of work, and increasingly found it in the houses of the English nobility. At Chatsworth, Derbyshire, being re-built towards the end of the century, both Louis Laguerre and Antonio Verrio painted flamboyant allegorical ceilings.

Seventeenth Century

S. Carlo alle Quatro Fontane, Rome, ITALY 1638. Borromini

Church of St Stephen, Walbrook, London, ENGLAND, 1672-87. Sir Christopher Wren

Royal staircase, Vatican Palace, Rome, ITALY. 1660-70. Bernini

Armoury, Hatfield House, Herts, ENGLAND. Originally an open arcade linking the two wings of the house at ground level. The openings were filled with stone tracery and glazed c.1830

Long Gallery, Haddon Hall, Derbyshire, ENGLAND. c.1600

Grand staircase, Hatfield House,
Herts, ENGLAND. 1607-11.
Robert Lyminge(?)

Great staircase, Knole, Kent,
ENGLAND. c.1604

Double cube room, Wilton House,
ENGLAND. Built to the designs
of Inigo Jones and completed 1653

Ceiling lunette over bed recess, King's bedroom,
castle of Vaux-le-Vicomte near Melun, FRANCE
1656-61. Le Vau and Le Brun

Plasterwork detail, Holyrood house,
SCOTLAND 1671

Room of the Queen's
guards, Versailles,
FRANCE 1670

Drawing room formerly the Hall, Western Park,
Shropshire, ENGLAND, after 1670

Great room, Palazzo
Colonna, Rome,
ITALY. completed
c.1670. Antonio del
Grande and Girolamo
Fontana.

Saloon, Belton House Grantham,
Lincolnshire, ENGLAND. 1684-7

Gallery of Hercules, Hotel Lambert,
Paris, FRANCE. c.1650-60

Main Hall, Town Hall, Amsterdam,
HOLLAND. 1648-65. Van Campen

Doorway, Gustav III's Bedroom,
Drottningholm Palace, SWEDEN.
c.1680

Chapel, Palace of Versailles,
FRANCE. 1689-1710. J. H.
Mansart

The painted hall, Chatsworth, Derbyshire, ENGLAND. 1687. William Talman.
The staircase was reconstructed in 1912. Painted decorations by Laguerre
1692-4

Eighteenth Century

The delicacy of the Rococo style is most appropriate to the small pavilions that were built in the huge landscaped parks of many European palaces in this century. They were elegant refuges where royalty and a few chosen courtiers could escape from the oppressive round of ritual and ceremony which court life involved. At the Nymphenburg Palace on the outskirts of Munich, which was used as a summer residence by the Elector, the Amalienburg is a tiny palace whose rooms were painted in pale colours with silvered plasterwork, while another pavilion is a very delightful bath-house. Many abbeys were re-built by their ambitious, usually nobly-born abbots in the most extravagant Rococo, with scenic effects in the churches derived from the contemporary theatre, as at Weltenburg Abbey, for instance.

The Rococo lingered on in Germany, especially at Potsdam, Prussia, where Frederick the Great continued to favour the style long after Neo-classicism made its appearance in France and England, although his study-bedroom was re-decorated in the year of his death in the new style.

In England the Baroque's late appearance was soon curtailed by a revival of the Palladian manner of Inigo Jones. The most influential member of the Palladian group was Lord Burlington, whose exquisite villa at Chiswick, London, is an epitome of the style, monumental in treatment even when small in scale. At Houghton Hall, Norfolk, by Colin Campbell, the gallery is based on the one at Chiswick, doubled in scale.

In Great Britain there are Neoclassical elements in the elaborate mannered work of the Adam brothers from Scotland, seen at its best at Kedleston Hall, Derbyshire, and Syon House, near London. A purer form of Neoclassicism is to be found in James Wyatt's early work at Heveningham Hall, Norfolk, and at Castle Coole, Ireland. Neoclassicism spread over the whole of Europe, to Poland, Russia, where another Scotsman, Charles Cameron, worked for Catherine the Great, Sweden and Spain.

In France a discerning patron of the arts like Madame de Pompadour encouraged the movement towards greater simplicity and purity of style. Gabriel's staircase at the Military School, Paris, anticipates the uncompromising bareness of Le Masson's palace for the Abbot of Royaumont.

Most Italian architects continued to build in a somewhat pompous form of late Baroque, but Filippo Juvarra in Piedmont rose above the general, admittedly high level of competence, in his church of the Superga and his hunting-lodge at Stupinigi, both near Turin. His staircase at the Madama Palace, Turin, rises up on two sides in a great light-filled space which occupies the whole height of the building.

Staircase, Easton Neston, Northants, ENGLAND. 1702. Hawksmoor

Antique passage, Castle Howard,
Yorkshire, ENGLAND. c.1700. Vanbrugh
and Hawksmoor

Great Hall, Blenheim Palace,
Oxfordshire, ENGLAND. Completed
1716. Vanbrugh

Long Library, Blenheim Palace.
Completed c.1725. Hawksmoor

Great Hall, Castle of Schleissheim, Munich,
GERMANY. 1725. Joseph Effner

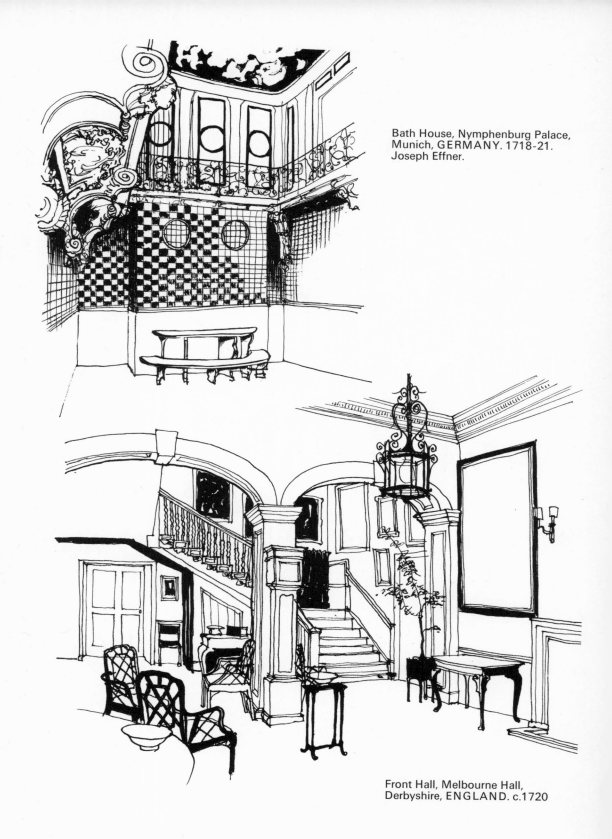

Bath House, Nymphenburg Palace,
Munich, GERMANY. 1718-21.
Joseph Effner.

Front Hall, Melbourne Hall,
Derbyshire, ENGLAND. c.1720

Staircase, Palace of Brühl,
Rhineland, GERMANY. 1743-8.
Balthaser Neumann

Choir, Abbey church, Weltenburg,
GERMANY 1717-21. The
Brothers Asam

The Gallery, Chiswick House, ENGLAND. 1725-9 Lord Burlington and William Kent

Gallery, Holkham Hall, Norfolk,
ENGLAND. 1734. William Kent

Chimney piece, Rushbrook Hall,
Suffolk, ENGLAND. 1740

Grand staircase, Military Academy,
Paris, FRANCE. 1751. Gabriele

Ballroom, Thurn and Taxis Palace,
Regensburg, GERMANY. 1730-40.
Transferred from Frankfurt in 1895

Staircase, Marble Palace, Potsdam,
GERMANY Late 18th cent.

Decoration detail, Hotel Lambert, Paris,
FRANCE Louis XVI. 1764-92

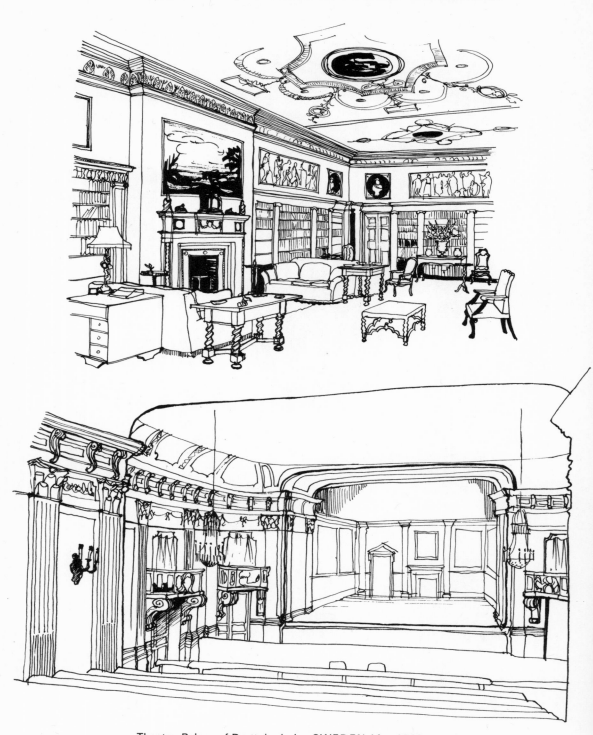

Library, Mellerstain, Berwickshire, SCOTLAND. 1770-8. Robert Adam

Theatre, Palace of Drottningholm, SWEDEN. After 1762

Hall, Kedleston Hall,
Derbyshire, ENGLAND
1760. Robert Adam

POSTERIS PRODESSE DIIS

Staircase, Liria Palace,
Madrid, SPAIN 1770
Rodriguez

Hall, Syon House, Middlesex,
ENGLAND. 1762 Robert Adam

Detail of white marble and ormulu
fireplace in Red Drawing Room

Library, Kenwood House, London,
ENGLAND. 1768 Robert Adam

Detail of white marble fireplace

Hall, Heveningham Hall,
Norfolk, ENGLAND. 1781.
James Wyatt

Etruscan room, Osterley
Park, Middlesex, ENGLAND.
1775. Robert Adam

The Salon, Castle Coole, Co. Fermanagh, IRELAND. 1788. James Wyatt

Lower Hall, The Abbott's Palace, Royaumont, FRANCE. 1789.
Louis Le Masson—a follower of Ledoux.

First floor hall, Abbott's Palace as opposite.

Marie Antoinette's bedroom, Petit Trianon, Versailles, FRANCE, 1174-6

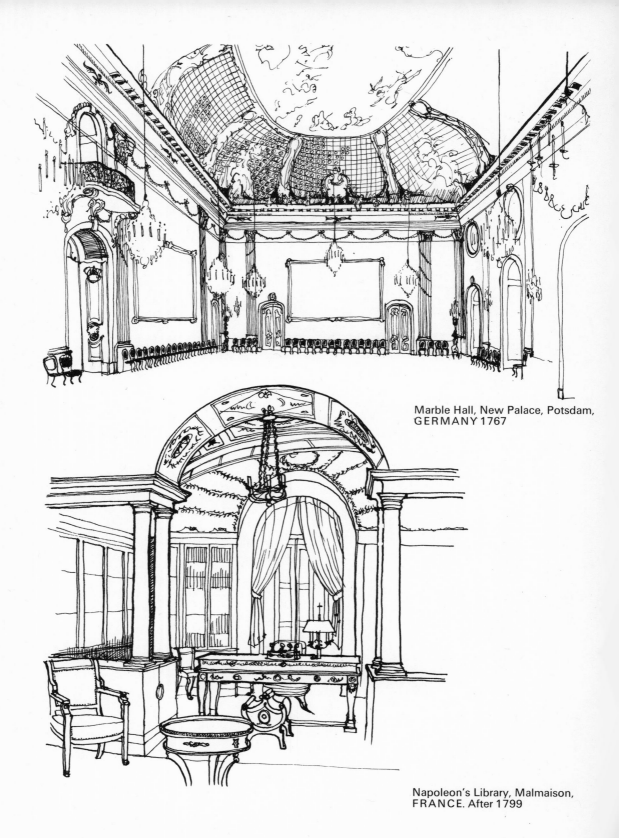

Marble Hall, New Palace, Potsdam,
GERMANY 1767

Napoleon's Library, Malmaison,
FRANCE. After 1799

Study Bedroom of Frederick the Great, Palace of Sans Souci, Potsdam, GERMANY.
1753. Erdmannsdorff

Ballroom at Lazienki, POLAND.
1790. Domenico Merlini

1st floor corridor, 475 Heerangracht,
Amsterdam, HOLLAND. c.1730
Probably designed by Daniel Marot

Nineteenth Century

The clean lines and uncluttered spaces of French Revolutionary Neo-classicism were not grand enough for Napoleon, who employed the brilliant decorators Percier and Fontaine to refurbish the palaces sacked during the Revolution in a style combining rich, strong colours and a profusion of classical detail of mainly Greek and Egyptian inspiration. The restoration of the Bourbon family made this Empire style politically undesirable, but a more florid version came back into fashion with Napoleon III in the 1850's and 1860's.

The revival of past styles is a characteristic of European design throughout most of the century. In England a wide variety can be found, including Louis XV at Apsley House, London, Gothic at Wilton House, Wiltshire, and Chinese at the Royal Pavilion, Brighton, Sussex, whose interior was the work of John Nash. The most distinguished architect of the early part of the century in England was Sir John Soane, who created a highly individual form of Neoclassicism that can still be appreciated in his London house, preserved as the Soane Museum. Nash had designed in any style required by his patrons, but A. W. Pugin who was responsible for the interiors at the new Houses of Parliament was a dedicated supporter of the revived Gothic style, which became much more truly medieval in spirit, as can be seen in the work of Alfred Waterhouse. William Morris, who mixed Pugin's Gothic with Marx's socialism, led the move in the direction of a domestic style based on the English country tradition. C. F. A. Voysey's sophisticated interiors have a beautiful, timeless quality.

The Art Nouveau style is seen at its best in public buildings such as restaurants and bars, where its affectations are stimulating.

Germany produced two great Neoclassical architects, C. F. Schinkel and Fredrich Gilly. The revivalist taste of the century can still be studied in the fantastic castles built for Ludwig II of Bavaria, a lonely, sensitive man who turned his dreams into buildings, as at Neuschwanstein, inspired by the world of Wagner's operas.

The most significant interior of the century was that of the Crystal Palace: this huge area enclosed by a prefabricated machine-made structure of iron, wood and glass indicated the real way ahead.

Nineteenth Century

Upper cloisters, Wilton House,
ENGLAND. Completed c.1814.
James Wyatt

Hall at Wilanow, Warsaw,
POLAND. Early 19th cent.

Waterloo Gallery, Apsley House, London, ENGLAND. 1829. Benjamin
Dean Wyatt. An unusual feature of the gallery's fittings is the sliding
mirror shutters, which can be drawn out of the walls to hide the windows
completely.

Banqueting room, Royal Pavilion,
Brighton, Sussex, ENGLAND.
1815. Nash

Eaton Hall, Cheshire, ENGLAND. 1867. Waterhouse

Library, Abbey of Klosterneuburg,
Vienna, AUSTRIA.1836-42.
Joseph Kornhäusel

Dining room chimney piece,
Cardiff castle, Glamorgan,
WALES. 1865. William Burges

Bon Marche Department store, Paris, FRANCE. 1876. Eiffel and Boileau

Crystal Palace, London, ENGLAND. 1851. Joseph Paxton

Salon, Ferrieres, Seine et Marne, FRANCE. c.1860. Built by Joseph Paxton, decorated by Eugene Almi

Opera House staircase, Paris, FRANCE. 1861-74. Charles Garnier

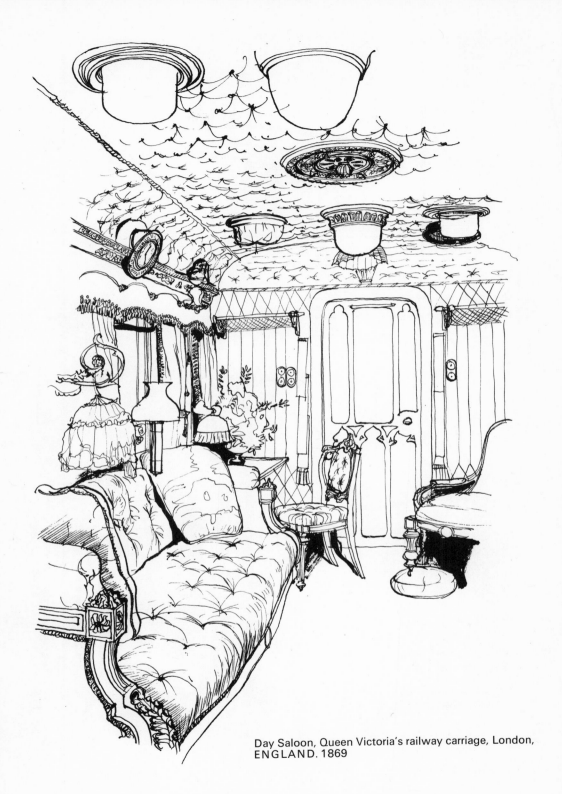

Day Saloon, Queen Victoria's railway carriage, London,
ENGLAND. 1869

Entrance Hall, Güell Palace, Barcelona, SPAIN 1885-8. Gaudi

Neuschwanstein castle, Bavaria, 1880. Right: Bedroom of Ludwig II. Left: the bed itself

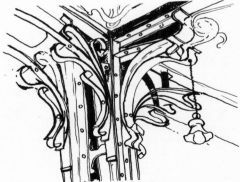

Below : light fitting detail

Van Eetvelde House, Brussels, BELGIUM. 1895
Victor Horta. Above : salon

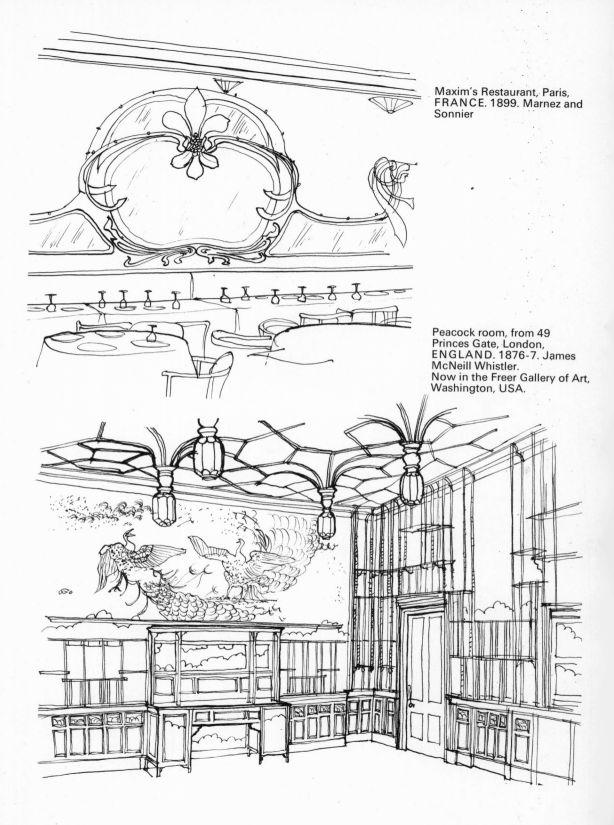

Maxim's Restaurant, Paris,
FRANCE. 1899. Marnez and
Sonnier

Peacock room, from 49
Princes Gate, London,
ENGLAND. 1876-7. James
McNeill Whistler.
Now in the Freer Gallery of Art,
Washington, USA.

La Vagenende Restaurant, Paris, FRANCE. c.1900

Dining room, Van Eetvelde House,
Brussels, BELGIUM. 1895. Victor
Horta

Door detail, Maxim's Restaurant,
Paris, FRANCE 1899. Marnez and
Sonnier

Library, Clouds, Wiltshire,
ENGLAND. 1880. Philip Webb

Breakfast Room, 13 Lincoln's Inn
Fields, London, ENGLAND. 1812.
Sir John Soane. Redecorated in 1951
to the original colours.

Smoking room, Aranjuez Palace, Madrid, SPAIN. c.1880.

Study in Jerome Doucet's house, Clamart, FRANCE. 1902.

Crypt of church of Coloma de Cervelló, Colonia Güell, SPAIN. begun 1898. Gaudi

Twentieth Century

The increasing role played by the state since the late nineteenth century has led to a great increase in the amount of institutional building. In 1907–9, C. R. Mackintosh, one of the leaders of the Art Nouveau movement, added a library to the Glasgow School of Art which he had designed ten years before. His style had hardened in the interval, and the line of development through the Dutch designers to the Bauhaus in Germany is already indicated. W. M. Dudok's Town Hall at Hilversum, Holland, is roughly contemporary with Walter Gropius's house at Dessau, Germany, which carries austerity almost as far as it can be taken without becoming clinical.

The tendency to strip away all ornamentation in this century has been mainly due to a strong reaction against the over-elaboration of much nineteenth-century decoration. Designers have become more responsive to influences from the colder countries, especially Scandinavia, where the use of materials in their natural state has always been a feature of popular, as opposed to court or aristocratic architecture. The most authoritative figure in European design today, Le Corbusier, has described a house as 'a machine for living'.

In England the modern style was slow to make its appearance, as the work of Sir Edwin Lutyens aptly illustrates. His neo-Baroque manner is still popular with more conservative patrons, for whom it represents the comfort and security of a fast vanishing style of living. The Festival of Britain in 1951 made modern architecture more acceptable in England, and did much to make the ordinary citizen aware of the importance of interior design.

Concrete, usually reinforced with steel rods, is the most widely used material of this century so far, and the achievements of the Italian P. L. Nervi since 1945 illustrate the tremendous progress that has been made in the exploitation of the possibilities of this material since Perret built his church at Le Raincy in the 1920's.

Stair Hall, Corn Exchange and Chamber of Commerce, Mantua,
ITALY, 1912. Aldus Andreani

Library, Glasgow School of
Art, SCOTLAND.1907-9
C. R. Mackintosh

Hall, Little Thakeham, Pulborough, Sussex,
ENGLAND. 1903. Edwin Lutyens.

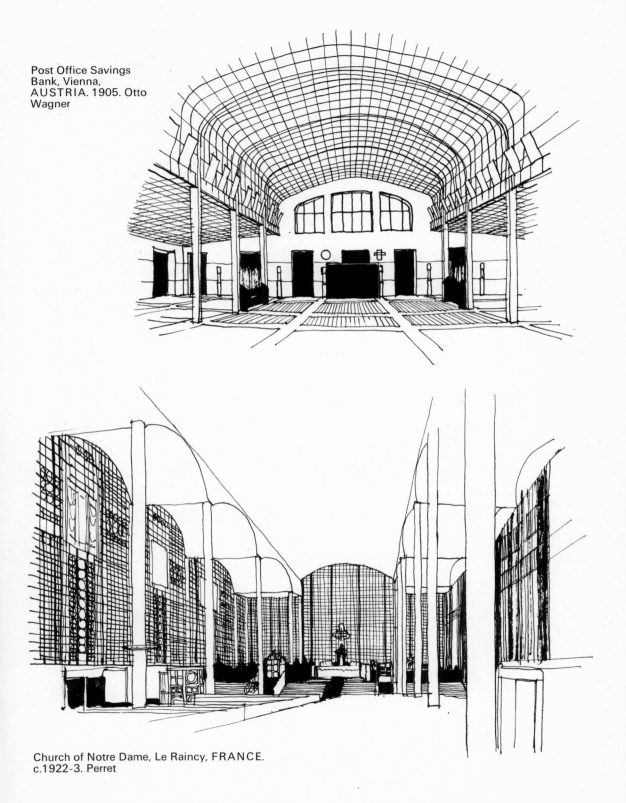

Post Office Savings Bank, Vienna, AUSTRIA. 1905. Otto Wagner

Church of Notre Dame, Le Raincy, FRANCE. c.1922-3. Perret

The Great Hall, Stock Exchange,
Amsterdam, Holland. 1898-1903.
H. P. Berlage

City Library, Stockholm,
SWEDEN. 1928.
Asplund

Marriage room, Town Hall, Hilversum, HOLLAND. 1928-30. W. M. Dudok

Factory, Hochst am Main, GERMANY. Peter Behrens

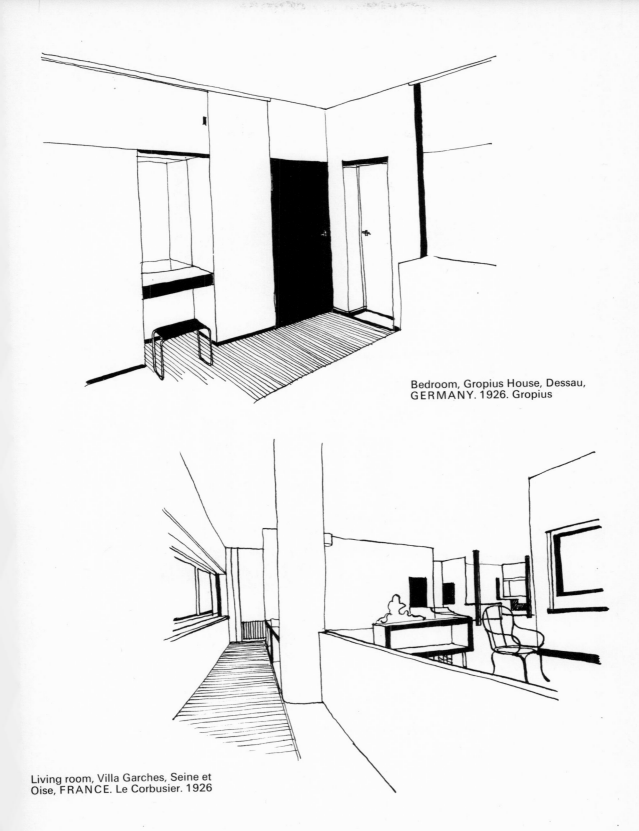

Bedroom, Gropius House, Dessau,
GERMANY. 1926. Gropius

Living room, Villa Garches, Seine et
Oise, FRANCE. Le Corbusier. 1926

Domestic Interior at Bordeaux, FRANCE. Le Corbusier

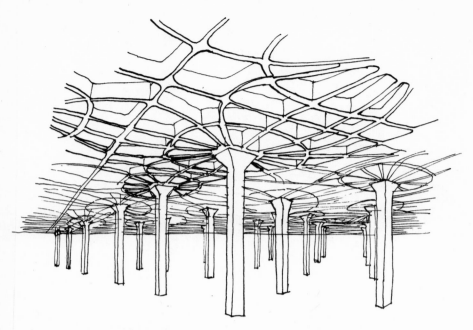

Gatti wool factory, Rome, ITALY. 1953. Nervi

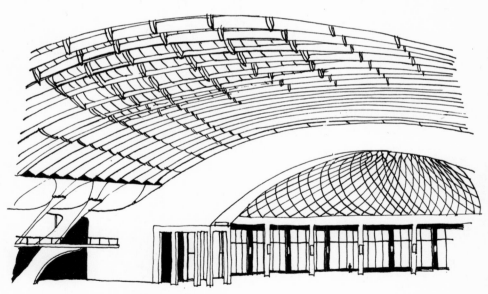

Exhibition Hall, Turin, ITALY. 1950. Nervi

Dining Hall, St Catherine's College, Oxford, ENGLAND. 1960-4.
Arne Jacobsen

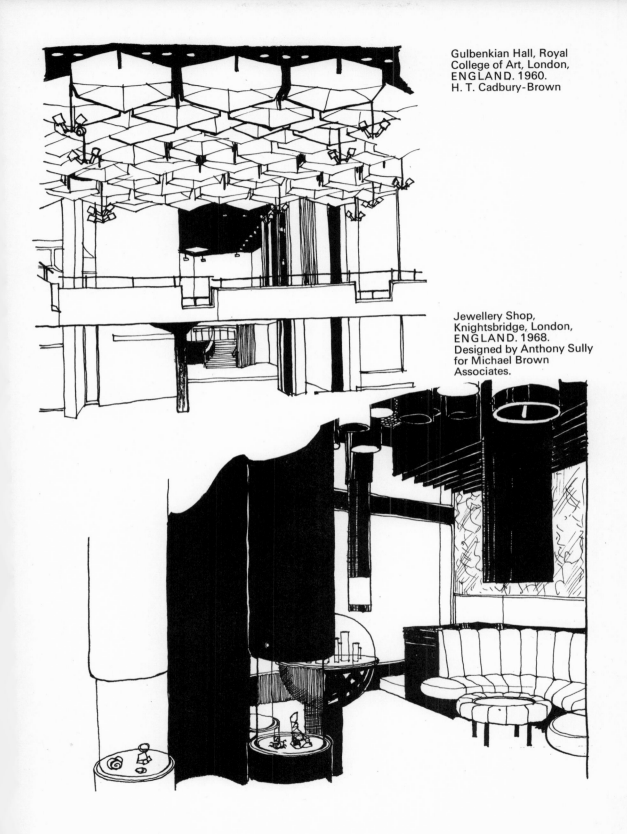

Gulbenkian Hall, Royal
College of Art, London,
ENGLAND. 1960.
H. T. Cadbury-Brown

Jewellery Shop,
Knightsbridge, London,
ENGLAND. 1968.
Designed by Anthony Sully
for Michael Brown
Associates.

Index

Abbey church 25, 79
Abbey of St Denis 33
Abbott's Palace 90
Adam, Robert 84, 85, 86, 87, 88
Almi, Eugene 101
Ambulatories 33
Amsterdam Town Hall 72
Andreani, Aldus 113
Angoulême Cathedral 30
Antique passage 76
Antoinette, Marie 91
Apsley House 97
Aranjuez Palace 110
Archivolt 31
Armoury 66
Arms of St Aubyn &
       Godolphin 54
Arnold, William 60
Asam, brothers 79
Asplund 116

Ballroom 82, 94
Barcelona Cathedral 37
Barn 45, 48
Baths 18
Bautista, Juan 57
Bedroom 91, 93, 104, 119
Behrens, Peter 118
Belton House 71
Berlage, H. P. 116
Bernini 65
Blenheim Palace 76, 77
Boileau 100
Bon Marche department store 100
Borromini 64
Breakfast room 109
Brown, Michael 123
Brühl Palace 79
Brun, Le 68
Brunelleschi 42
Burges, William 99
Burgos Cathedral 46
Burlington, Lord 80
Bussert, Martin 59

Cadbury-Brown 123
Campen, Van 72
Canterbury Cathedral 30
Capitals 24, 30, 35
   Greek 16
Caravanserai 15
Cardiff Castle 99

Carriage, railway 103
Castle Coole 89
Castle Howard 76
Catacomb 20
Ceiling lunette 68
Chamber of Commerce 113
Chambord 56
Chapel 27, 42, 45, 46, 72
Chapter House 38, 47
Chateaudun 57
Chatsworth 73
Chevy Chase 54
Chimney piece 81, 99
Chiswick House 80
Cloisters 28
Cloister door 31
Clouds 109
Coloma de Corvelló 111
Compton Wynyates 52
Corbusier, Le 119, 120
Corn Exchange 113
Corridor 94
Crathes Castle 55
Cross vaults 29
Crypt 111
Crystal Palace 100

Dining pavilion 17
   room 108
Domestic interior 120
Double Cube room 68
Doucet, Jerome 111
Drawing room 70
Drottningholm 72, 84
Ducal Palace 43
Dudok, W. M. 117
Durham Cathedral 26

Easton Neston 75
Eaton Hall 98
Eetvelde, Van, House 105, 108
Effner, Joseph 77, 78
Eiffel 100
Egeskov 59
Encaustic tile 38
Erdmannsdorff 93
Escorial 57
Etruscan room 88
Exchange, the Lonja 46
Exeter Cathedral 39
Exhibition Hall 121

Factory 118
Ferrieres 101
Fiorentino 56
Fireplace 86, 87
Fontainbleau 56
Fontana, Girolamo 70
Frederick the Great 93
Funeral chapel 20

Gabriele 82
Gallery 35, 56, 80, 81
Gallery & Pulpit 35
Garches villa 119
Garnier, Charles 102
Gatehouse tower 47
Gatti wool factory 121
Gaudi 104, 111
Glasgow School of Art 114
Gloucester Cathedral 40
Grande, Antonio del 70
Great Dixter 49
Gropius 119
Güell Palace 104
Gulbenkian Hall 123

Haddon Hall 66
Hadrian 17, 18, 19
Hall of Swans 58
Hardwick Hall 53
Hatfield House 66, 67
Hawksmoor 75, 76, 77
Heerangracht (No. 475) 94
Hercules Gallery 71
Herrera, Juan de 57
Heveningham Hall 88
Hillside Farm 50
Hochst am Main 118
Holkham Hall 81
Holyrood House 69
Hontañòn, Juan Gil de 47
Horta, Victor 105, 108
Hotel Lambert 71, 83

Ightham Mote 40

Jacobsen, Arne 122
Jewellery Shop 123
Jones, Inigo 68

Kedleston Hall 85
Kent, William 80, 81
Kenwood House 87
King's College Chapel 45
King's Chamber 47
Kitchen 50, 62
Klosterneuburg Abbey 99
Knole 67
Knossos 15

Kornhäusel, Joseph 99
Kronberg 59

Laguerre 73
Laon Cathedral 35
Lascaux 14
Lazienki 94
Leptis Magna 18
Library 60, 84, 87, 99, 109, 116
Light fitting 105
Lincoln's Inn Fields 13, 109
Liria Palace 85
Little Thakeham 114
Long Gallery 55, 66
Longleat House 53
Lonja, the 46
Lutyens, Edwin 114
Lyminge, Robert 67

Mackintosh 114
Madonna and child 42
Magdalene 29
Malmaison 92
Mansart, J. H. 72
Marble Hall 92
Maria Leach 29
Marnex 106, 108
Marot, Daniel 94
Marriage room 117
Masson, Louis Le 90
Maxim's Restaurant 106, 108
Melbourne Hall 78
Mellerstain 84
Merlini, Domenico 94
Michelangelo 60
Military Academy 82
Minstrel's gallery 52
Modena Cathedral 35
Montacute 60
Mosaic details 22
Mosque, Cordova 24

Napoleon's Library 92
Nash 98
Neolithic House 14
Nervi 121
Neumann, Balthaser 79
Neuschwanstein Castle 104
New Cathedral, Salamanca 47
Notre Dame 115
Nymphenburg Palace 78

Opera House 102
Orders—
    Greek 16
    Roman 17
Osterley Park 88
Oxburgh Hall 47

Painted Hall 73
Palazzo Colonna 70
Palladio 61
Pantheon, Rome 19
Paxton 100, 101
Pazzi chapel 42
Peacock room 106
Perret 115
Petit Trianon 91
Philip II's apartment 57
Plasterwork 69
Post Office 115
Potsdam—
    New Palace 92
    Sans Souci 93
    Marble Palace 83

Queen's Megaron 15

Ravenna 22
Red Drawing Room 86
Rodriguez 85
Rosselino, Antonio 42
Royal College of Art 123
Royal Pavilion, Banqueting room 98
Royal staircase, Vatican 65
Royaumont, The Abbott's Palace 90, 91
Rushbrook Hall 81

Salisbury Cathedral 38
Salon 43, 89, 101, 105
Saloon 71
Sans Souci 93
Schleissheim Castle 77
Sens Cathedral 34
Siena Cathedral 36
Simon of Cologne 46
Sintra Palace 58
Smoking room 110
Smythson, Robert 53
Soane, Sir John 109
Sonnier 106, 108
Stock Exchange 116
Stone screen 60
Study 111
Study Bedroom 93
Sully, Anthony 123
Syon House 86
S. Appollinare Nuovo 22
S. Carlo alle Quattro Fontane 64
S. Catherine's College 122

S. Constanza 20
S. Croce 42
S. Cyriacus 25
S. Domingo de Silos 28
S. Emmeram 31
S. Front 31
S. Giorgio Maggiore 61
S. John's Chapel 27
S. Larenzo 23, 60
S. Maria Maggiore 21
S. Michael's Mount 54
S. Miniato al Monte 36
S. Nicholas de Port 45
S. Pietro 28
S. Savin-sur-Gartempe 29
S. Spirito 42
S. Stephen 65

Talman, William 73
Temple of Aphaia 16
Theatre 84
Thurn and Taxis Palace 82
Tower of London 27
Town Hall 117
Tratzberg Castle 62
Tympanum 29

Vagenende, La 107
Vanbrugh 76
Vatican 65
Vau, Le 68
Vaux-le-comte 68
Versaille 69, 72
Via Latina 20
Victoria, Queen 103
Vignola 62
Villa Lante 62
Vitale 24

Wagner, Otto 115
Walksoken church 33
Waterhouse 98
Waterloo Gallery 97
Webb, Philip 109
Western Park 70
Westminster Abbey, floor 38
Westwork 25
Whistler, J. M. 106
Wilanow 96
Wilton House 68, 96
Wren, Sir Christopher 65
Wyatt, Benjamin Dean 97
Wyatt, James 88, 89, 96